COUNTRIES

# GUATEMALA

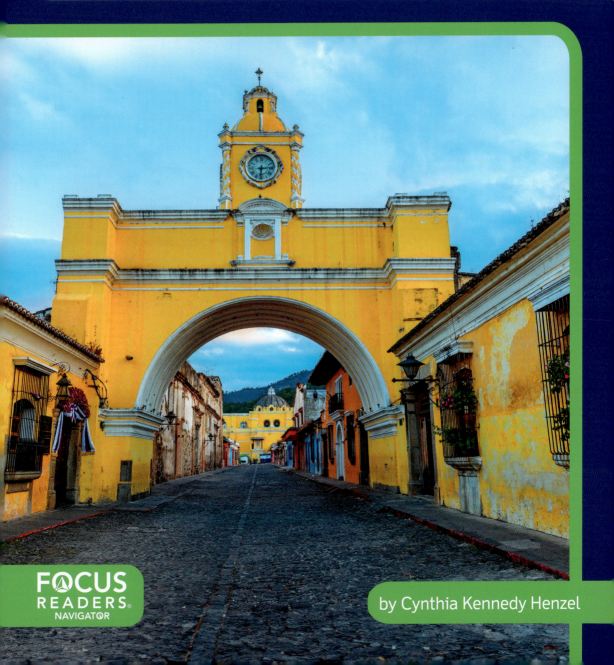

by Cynthia Kennedy Henzel

FOCUS READERS®
NAVIGATOR

# WWW.FOCUSREADERS.COM

Copyright © 2025 by Focus Readers®, Mendota Heights, MN 55120. All rights reserved. No part of this book may be reproduced or utilized in any form or by any means without written permission from the publisher.

Focus Readers is distributed by North Star Editions:
sales@northstareditions.com | 888-417-0195

Produced for Focus Readers by Red Line Editorial.

Content Consultant: Alvis E. Dunn, PhD, Associate Professor of History, University of North Carolina Asheville

Photographs ©: Shutterstock Images, cover, 1, 4–5, 14–15, 20–21, 22, 25, 26–27, 28; Red Line Editorial, 6; iStockphoto, 8–9, 16, 19; Bettmann/Getty Images, 11; Luis Soto/AP Images, 13

**Library of Congress Cataloging-in-Publication Data**
Names: Henzel, Cynthia Kennedy, 1954- author.
Title: Guatemala / by Cynthia Kennedy Henzel.
Description: Mendota Heights, MN: Focus Readers, [2025] | Series: Countries | Includes bibliographical references and index. | Audience: Grades 4-6
Identifiers: LCCN 2024029716 (print) | LCCN 2024029717 (ebook) | ISBN 9798889982234 (hardcover) | ISBN 9798889982791 (paperback) | ISBN 9798889983859 (pdf) | ISBN 9798889983354 (ebook)
Subjects: LCSH: Guatemala--Juvenile literature.
Classification: LCC F1463.2 .H45 2025  (print) | LCC F1463.2  (ebook) | DDC 972.81--dc23/eng/20240807
LC record available at https://lccn.loc.gov/2024029716
LC ebook record available at https://lccn.loc.gov/2024029717

Printed in the United States of America
Mankato, MN
012025

## ABOUT THE AUTHOR
Cynthia Kennedy Henzel has a BS in social studies education and an MS in geography. She has worked as a teacher-educator in many countries. Currently, she writes fiction and nonfiction books and develops education materials for social studies, history, science, and ELL students. She has written more than 100 books and more than 150 stories for young people.

# TABLE OF CONTENTS

**CHAPTER 1**
**Welcome to Guatemala** 5

**CHAPTER 2**
**History** 9

**CHAPTER 3**
**Climate, Plants, and Animals** 15

**CLIMATE CRISIS IN GUATEMALA**
**Failing Farms** 18

**CHAPTER 4**
**Resources, Economy, and Government** 21

**CHAPTER 5**
**People and Culture** 27

Focus Questions • 30
Glossary • 31
To Learn More • 32
Index • 32

**CHAPTER 1**

# WELCOME TO GUATEMALA

Guatemala is a land of mountains, forests, lakes, and beaches. The country is located in Central America. Guatemala shares borders with four countries. Belize and Mexico are to the north. Honduras and El Salvador are to the east. The Pacific Ocean is to the

Guatemala's highest mountain is a volcano called Tajumulco. It rises up 13,845 feet (4,220 m).

south. In the east, Guatemala touches the Caribbean Sea.

Mountains divide Guatemala into three regions. The Highlands region is in the center. This area has many lakes and valleys. Most people live in this part of

the country. Guatemala City, the capital and largest city, is here. The area is also home to many **Indigenous** communities.

The Pacific Coast region is to the south. A line of volcanoes separates it from the Highlands. Guatemala has more than 20 volcanoes. Three are still active. They are Santiaguito, Fuego, and Pacaya. The Pacific Coast's land is low and flat. Its plains have rich soil.

More lowlands are in the north. This region is called Petén. It covers approximately one-third of the country. But few people live there. Instead, Petén has hills and rainforests. Many famous Maya ruins are there, too.

**CHAPTER 2**

# HISTORY

The Maya have lived in Guatemala for thousands of years. At first, they had small farms and villages. But by 200 BCE, they had built an empire with many large cities. Around 900 CE, the Maya began leaving their cities. But villages remained.

The Spanish invaded Guatemala in the 1500s. They made it a **colony**. They

Tikal began as a small Maya village. By 600 CE, it was home to more than 10,000 people.

brought enslaved workers from Africa to grow cacao, indigo, and other products on large farms.

Guatemala stayed under Spanish rule until 1821. After that, its government changed several times. Guatemala became fully independent in 1839. Rafael Carrera was its first leader. He ruled as a dictator until his death. In 1871, Justo Rufino Barrios helped lead a revolution. He eventually became president. He tried to make Guatemala more modern. He improved roads and education. And he made coffee a key crop.

After Barrios, the government struggled. In 1931, General Jorge Ubico

Soldiers parade in front of the palace where Jorge Ubico lived. As president, he had nearly unlimited control.

seized power. He focused on making Guatemala richer. But his strict rule often limited people's rights. In 1944, workers held a **strike**. They forced Ubico to resign.

The country's next leaders focused on helping workers. For example, Jacobo Arbenz supported a 1952 law. It said unused land from large properties could be given to farmers. A US company owned much of Guatemala's land. The company asked US leaders to act. They helped train soldiers who forced Arbenz to step down. More unrest followed.

By 1960, civil war had begun. **Guerrilla** fighters opposed the new government. Many Indigenous people supported these

## RIGOBERTA MENCHÚ

Rigoberta Menchú is an activist who helped end Guatemala's civil war. Menchú is from a Maya people called the K'iche'. During the war, government forces killed her parents and brother. Menchú called for an end to the violence. She won a Nobel Peace Prize in 1992. And she continues speaking out for the rights of Indigenous peoples.

Rigoberta Menchú had to flee Guatemala because of her family's work as activists.

fighters. So, the government sent soldiers to destroy Maya villages and crops. More than 200,000 people died.

A peace agreement ended the war in 1996. But problems with violence and government **corruption** continued.

**CHAPTER 3**

# CLIMATE, PLANTS, AND ANIMALS

Weather in Guatemala tends to be warm and wet. However, the **climate** varies throughout the country. That's because the land's elevation changes so much. Low-lying areas stay warmer. High in the mountains, weather becomes cool.

The country has a dry season from November to April. Then a rainy season

More than 8,000 types of plants grow throughout Guatemala's varied landscape.

The resplendent quetzal lives in cloud forests. These forests are warm and wet.

lasts from May to October. Much of this rain falls along mountain slopes. Valleys beyond these slopes stay much drier.

Guatemala has many types of forests. The coast has mangroves. Rainforests cover much of Petén. Pines and oaks grow on mountains. However, many trees across the country have been cut down.

Thousands of different plants and animals live in Guatemala. Many live nowhere else in the world. The Maya mouse is one example. Guatemala's forests are also home to birds, monkeys, and big cats.

## RESPLENDENT QUETZAL

The resplendent quetzal is Guatemala's national bird. The male's tail has long, colorful feathers. The Maya once used these feathers like money. Today, Guatemala's money is called the quetzal. Wild quetzals are in danger. Many forests have been destroyed. So, people set aside areas for the birds to live.

> **CLIMATE CRISIS IN GUATEMALA**

# FAILING FARMS

Guatemala is among the countries most at risk because of **climate change**. Many people in Guatemala are farmers. They grow crops for food and money. However, climate change can affect an area's rainfall. In some cases, it makes droughts worse. Other times, it can bring strong storms and flooding. Both can be devastating for farmers. Without rain, crops die. But floods bury crops and sweep away soil.

If crops fail, people can starve. By 2021, more than 20 percent of people in Guatemala struggled to get enough food. People also struggled to find work. Large farms are a main source of jobs in Guatemala. The farms hire people to pick crops. But when crops fail, these workers aren't needed.

People may have to leave their land if they are unable to work or grow food. Some try to go to other countries. However, this process can be

In Guatemala's mountainous areas, many people rely on small farms for food.

difficult. Some people travel to Petén. They try to start farms there instead. To do this, they may cut down the region's forests.

CHAPTER 4

# RESOURCES, ECONOMY, AND GOVERNMENT

Guatemala's main resources are farmland and forests. Large farms grow sugarcane, palm oil, coffee, and bananas. These crops are sold to other countries. Subsistence farmers grow food such as corn and beans for their families.

Guatemala's forests supply timber. Rare trees such as rosewood are especially

Coffee beans are dried in the sun after being picked from trees.

At El Mirador National Park in northern Guatemala, visitors can see ruins of Maya buildings.

valuable. Their wood is used to make musical instruments and furniture. Other trees supply rubber or chicle, which is used in some chewing gums. Many people use wood to cook and heat their homes. **Hydropower** is another main energy source.

Tourism is a major industry in Guatemala. Every year, many people visit.

They enjoy the country's natural beauty. They also see the ruins of ancient Maya cities. Tikal is one of the most famous. The ancient city was home to thousands of people. Many of its houses, temples, and palaces are still standing.

Today, a president leads Guatemala's government. The country also has a

## ANTIGUA GUATEMALA

Many tourists visit the ruins of Antigua Guatemala. The Spanish built this city in the 1520s. It was their colony's capital. In 1773, an earthquake almost destroyed it. The Spanish moved their capital to Guatemala City. But people rebuilt Antigua Guatemala. Today, it has many famous old buildings.

congress. People vote to elect these leaders. But the government has high levels of corruption. This causes many problems for Guatemala's people. Most of the country's money goes to rich people who live in cities. In rural areas, many people face poverty. Indigenous people are more likely to live in rural places. They are also more likely to be victims of crimes. Getting justice can be difficult. Government leaders often accept bribes or work with criminals. People who speak out about this problem are often jailed or killed.

Corrupt leaders even use their power to control judges and elections. In 2023,

People gather near city hall in Antigua Guatemala to protest corruption in 2017.

Bernardo Arévalo ran for president. He promised to fight corruption. Other leaders didn't want him to win. So, they tried to **suspend** his political party. They failed. Arévalo still won. But the event drew outrage in Guatemala and around the world. People called for an end to the corruption.

25

**CHAPTER 5**

# PEOPLE AND CULTURE

Guatemala has a population of about 18 million. Approximately 40 percent of the country's residents are Indigenous. The majority are Maya. Others are Xinca or Garifuna. Other residents are known as Ladinos. They have a mix of Spanish and Indigenous **ancestry**.

Maya women have used looms to create beautiful fabric for thousands of years.

Masked dancers and marimba players perform songs that blend Maya and Spanish influences.

Spanish is Guatemala's official language. But people also speak many Indigenous languages. For example, there are more than 20 different Maya groups. Each has its own language and customs.

Maya culture is a key part of life in Guatemala. People grow traditional foods such as corn, chilies, black beans, and squash. They also make beautiful art. People spin yarn from cotton. They dye it and weave it into cloth. The colors and patterns show where a person is from.

Approximately half of Guatemalans are under 19. Many of these young people are working for change. So are newer leaders. Both groups aim to lessen corruption.

## MAKING MUSIC

The marimba is an instrument made of wood bars. It is originally from Africa. But enslaved workers introduced it to Guatemala. It became a key part of Maya culture. In the 1900s, Guatemala's government attacked both the Maya and their customs. However, people kept playing marimba. Today, it is Guatemala's national instrument.

# FOCUS QUESTIONS

*Write your answers on a separate piece of paper.*

**1.** Write a paragraph describing some of Guatemala's natural resources.

**2.** Which part of Guatemala would you most like to visit? Why?

**3.** In what year did Guatemala become fully independent?
- **A.** 1821
- **B.** 1839
- **C.** 1921

**4.** What could happen if a country's government became less corrupt?
- **A.** More money could reach poor people, who need it.
- **B.** More money could go to just a few rich people.
- **C.** The country's leaders could keep more money for themselves.

*Answer key on page 32.*

# GLOSSARY

**ancestry**
Family members from the past.

**climate**
The average weather conditions of a particular area.

**climate change**
A human-caused global crisis involving long-term changes in Earth's temperature and weather patterns.

**colony**
An area controlled by a country that is far away.

**corruption**
Dishonest or illegal acts, especially by powerful people.

**guerrilla**
Using small groups to carry out surprise attacks.

**hydropower**
Using running water to produce electricity.

**Indigenous**
Native to a region, or belonging to ancestors who lived in a region before colonists arrived.

**strike**
When people stop working as a way to demand better working conditions or better pay.

**suspend**
To stop a group from being able to work.

# TO LEARN MORE

## BOOKS

Dickmann, Nancy. *Your Passport to Guatemala*. North Mankato, MN: Capstone Publishing, 2021.

Finan, Catherine C. *The Maya Civilization*. Minneapolis: Bearport Publishing, 2022.

Lassieur, Allison. *Maya Civilization*. Mendota Heights, MN: Focus Readers, 2020.

## NOTE TO EDUCATORS

Visit **www.focusreaders.com** to find lesson plans, activities, links, and other resources related to this title.

# INDEX

Antigua Guatemala, 6, 23
Arbenz, Jacobo, 11–12
Arévalo, Bernardo, 25

Barrios, Justo Rufino, 10

Carrera, Rafael, 10
civil war, 12–13
climate change, 18
corruption, 13, 24–25, 29
crops, 10, 13, 18, 21

forests, 5, 7, 16–17, 19, 21

Garifuna, 27

Highlands, 6–7

Ladinos, 27

Maya people, 9, 12–13, 17, 27–29
Menchú, Rigoberta, 12
mountains, 5–6, 15–17

Pacific Coast, 6–7
Petén, 6–7, 16, 19

Spanish, 9–10, 23, 27

Tikal, 23

Ubico, Jorge, 10–11

volcanoes, 6–7

Xinca, 27

Answer Key: 1. Answers will vary; 2. Answers will vary; 3. B; 4. A